13.01

Crabapples

Why do Animals do that?

Bobbie Kalman & Greg Nickles

Crabtree Publishing Company

Crabapples

created by Bobbie Kalman

For Stephanie Nickles, with love

Editor-in-Chief
Bobbie Kalman

Writing team
Bobbie Kalman
Greg Nickles

Managing editor
Lynda Hale

Editors
Niki Walker
Petrina Gentile

Computer design
Lynda Hale

Color separations and film
Dot 'n Line Image Inc.

Printer
Worzalla Publishing Company

Illustrations
Barbara Bedell

Photographs
Animals Animals: Henry Ausloos: page 30; G.I. Bernard: pages 18, 20;
 Ken Cole: page 9; J.A.L. Cooke: page 24 (bottom right);
 Stephen Dalton: pages 4-5; Zig Leszczynski: pages 28 (left), 29 (left);
 James E. Lloyd: page 11 (bottom); Joe McDonald: page 28 (right);
 Colin Milkins: page 17 (bottom); Fritz Prenzel: page 27;
 Richard Schiell: page 16; Stouffer Prod.: page 7; Leen Vander Silk:
 page 17 (top)
Frank S. Balthis: page 24 (top)
Joe B. Blossom/Photo Researchers, Inc.: page 6
John Daly: pages 8-9, 11 (top)
Jeff Foott: page 26
David Gilchrist: page 21
Wolfgang Kaehler: page 19
Bobbie Kalman: page 29 (right)
James Kamstra: pages 15, 25 (bottom left)
Linda Menzies: page 10 (top)
Tom Stack & Associates: Nancy Adams: cover; Thomas Kitchin:
 title page; Joe & Carol McDonald: pages 12-13; Joe McDonald:
 pages 10 (bottom), 23; Wendy Shattil & Bob Rozinski: page 14;
 Roy Toft: page 22

Crabtree Publishing Company

350 Fifth Avenue	360 York Road, RR 4,	73 Lime Walk
Suite 3308	Niagara-on-the-Lake,	Headington
New York	Ontario, Canada	Oxford OX3 7AD
N.Y. 10118	L0S 1J0	United Kingdom

Cataloging in Publication Data

Kalman, Bobbie
 Why do animals do that?

(Crabapples)
Includes index.

ISBN 0-86505-636-6 (library bound) ISBN 0-86505-736-2 (pbk.)
Why animals hibernate, use tools, imprint, and change color
are some of the questions answered in this book.

1. Animal behavior - Miscellanea - Juvenile literature. I. Nickles,
Greg, 1969- . II. Title. III. Series: Kalman, Bobbie. Crabapples.

QL751.5.K34 1996   j591.51   LC 96-43341
                                                    CIP

What is in this book?

Why do animals do that?

Have you ever wondered why animals behave the way they do? Some animals sleep all winter long. Others change their colors. Some pretend they are dead, and some have a terrible smell! Maybe you have seen, read, or heard about a creature doing something you think is beautiful, funny, or disgusting.

Scientists study **animal behavior** to understand why animals do things that seem unusual to humans. They have discovered that animals use their special abilities to get food, protect themselves, find mates, avoid enemies, or survive in harsh weather. Animals do the things they do to stay alive!

4

Why do animals hibernate?

Food is easy to find during the summer, but it is not always available during the cold northern winter. To keep from starving, some animals fall into a deep sleep called **hibernation**.

During hibernation, an animal's heart-beat and breathing slow down, and its body temperature drops close to freezing. The animal uses very little energy. It may sleep for weeks or just a few hours.

Some types of squirrels, groundhogs, bats, frogs, toads, and hedgehogs are **true hibernators**. Bears do not actually hibernate. They fall into a deep winter sleep, but their body temperature drops very little.

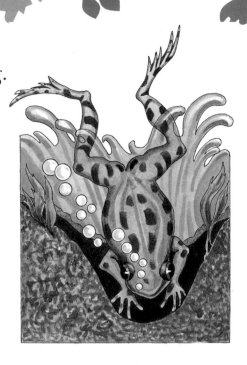

Why do animals migrate?

Some animals survive the winter by **migrating**, or traveling long distances in search of food and warmer weather. Animals also migrate to find water or a safe place to breed. Most are born knowing when and where to go.

Many fish, mammals, insects, and birds migrate thousands of kilometers each year. Monarch butterflies can be seen migrating between Canada, California, and Mexico. There are so many that they cover entire trees when they stop to rest!

Why do animals change color?

Many animals have colors and patterns that are the same as their surroundings. This disguise, called **camouflage**, helps them avoid being spotted by **predators**, the animals that eat them. Camouflage also helps predators hide so that they can surprise their prey.

Some animals, such as the chameleon and octopus, can change their skin color. This ability helps them hide in different surroundings.

The chameleon and octopus also seem to change color depending on the temperature, the amount of daylight, or their mood. Scientists do not know the reasons for these color changes.

Why do animals mimic?

When an animal acts, sounds, or looks like something else, it is **mimicking** that animal or object. Many creatures mimic in order to hide, scare away predators, or lure prey.

Can you see a difference between this viceroy butterfly and the monarchs on page 8? Viceroys mimic monarchs to keep from being eaten by birds. Even though the viceroy is tasty, birds avoid eating it because they mistake it for the poisonous monarch.

A predatory female firefly mimics the mating flashes of other fireflies. When the predator lures a male firefly, she catches and eats him!

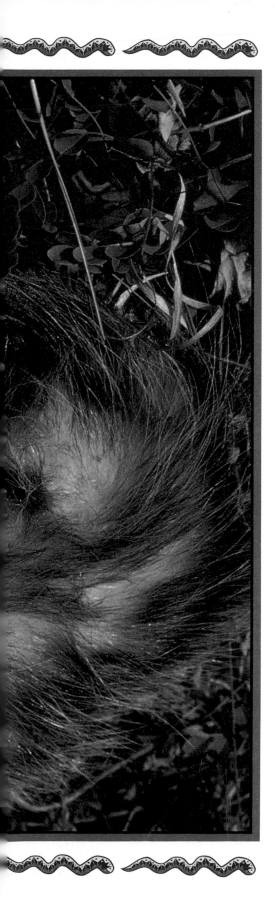

Why do animals play dead?

Have you ever seen an opossum playing dead? It curls up on the ground, and its body goes limp. Its eyes look glassy and lifeless, and its pink tongue hangs out of its mouth!

Opossums and other animals, such as the hognosed snake and pale prominent moth, play dead to avoid being eaten by predators. Most predators will not eat an animal unless they kill it themselves. When a predator threatens an opossum, the opossum falls unconscious. It does not move or make a sound and looks as if it has died.

The act usually fools the predator, which walks away without harming the opossum. A few minutes after the predator has left, the opossum wakes up, "returning to life."

Why do animals smell bad?

All animals have their own smell, or **scent**. An animal's scent may identify its family, mark its territory, or attract a mate. Some animals even use their scent to protect themselves from enemies.

Skunks produce a strong-smelling liquid called **musk**. Musk is made and stored in **glands** near the skunk's tail. When another animal comes too close, the skunk raises its tail and sprays musk from its glands. While the intruder is reeling from the powerful odor, the skunk runs away.

A stinky scent is also part of the hognosed snake's defenses. To fool predators, this snake curls up and plays dead. To make its act convincing, it releases an odor like that of a dead, rotting animal.

Why do animals live off others?

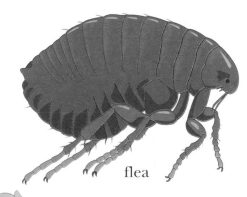
flea

A **parasite** is an animal that lives off another living creature, called a **host**. Parasites make their homes on or inside a creature's body and feed on its blood or flesh. Eventually, they may cause their host to die. Parasites, such as fleas, ticks, and flukes, feed on every kind of animal, including humans. Even small creatures, such as the daddy longlegs above, can be hosts to tiny parasites like these mites!

Why do animals depend on each other?

Symbiosis is a partnership between creatures of different species. Each animal helps the other survive. The oxpecker is a bird that pecks harmful parasites from the bodies of large animals. In return, the oxpecker feasts on the pests it pecks.

Aphids make a sweet syrup from plant sap, which ants use for food. To get a steady supply of syrup, some ants keep aphids in the same way farmers keep cows. They "herd" the aphids, making sure they get lots of plant sap to eat.

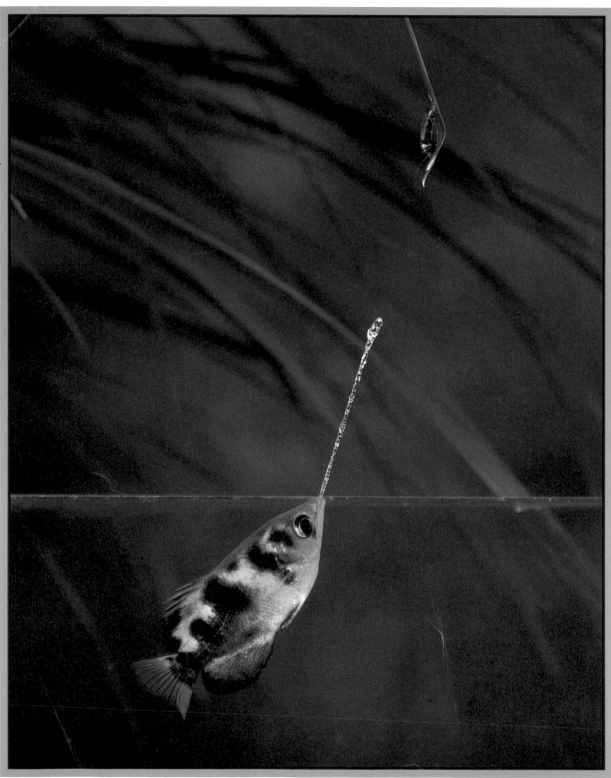

Why do animals spit?

Spitting may seem rude to humans, but it is important for the survival of some animals. The archer fish spits from below the water's surface to "shoot" at insects above. When the prey is hit, it falls into the water, where the archer fish gobbles it up.

Camels spit to scare away enemies and other camels. The humpless guanaco, below, is well known for its awful spit. An angry guanaco pulls back its ears, lifts its head, and snorts loudly. The powerful snorts cause a mixture of water, food, and mucus to spray out.

Why do animals make their own light?

Have you ever seen an animal that glows in the dark? Many creatures, especially those living in deep waters, produce a natural glow. A creature's ability to light up is called **bioluminescence**. A chemical reaction happens in the body of bioluminescent animals. The light produced can be a variety of colors. Unlike the hot light from an electric bulb, bioluminescent light is very cool.

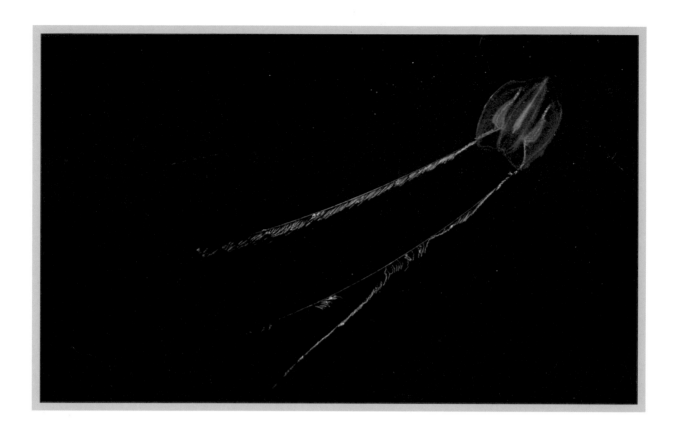

In bioluminescent insects, such as the firefly and click beetle, the chemical reaction occurs inside special organs called **lanterns**. Many insects flash their lanterns to attract mates.

Some bioluminescent animals use their glow to confuse predators. Other creatures, such as the comb jelly shown above, use their bioluminescent light to lure the tiny sea creatures on which they feed.

Why do animals like dirt?

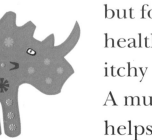

Playing in the mud or dirt can be fun, but for many animals it is a way to stay healthy. A roll in the dirt can ease an itchy back or cause parasites to jump off. A mud bath protects an animal's skin and helps it cool off during hot weather.

An elephant, hippopotamus, rhinoceros, or pig may spend the entire day wading in a mud hole. Wet mud adds moisture to the animal's skin and keeps it from drying out and cracking. When the mud dries, it forms a thick layer through which insects cannot bite.

A type of beetle called a scarab sculpts animal dung into huge balls. It rolls the balls into its burrow and uses them as food and a place to lay eggs. When the young scarab **larvae** hatch from the eggs, they also eat the dung.

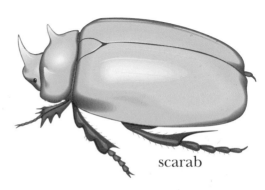

scarab

Why do animals imprint?

The world is a dangerous place for baby animals. If they become separated from their parent, they lose their guardian, source of food, and teacher. It is very important that baby animals know their parents. Learning to recognize parents is called **imprinting**.

Scientists believe that many types of animals imprint when they are very young. Some parents repeatedly make a sound or touch their baby in a way it learns to recognize. Some babies do not need this kind of help, however. They memorize the appearance or movements of the first thing they see.

Most animal babies imprint on their mother, but some imprint on another animal if their mother is not around. The story of the Ugly Duckling is about a cygnet that imprints on a duck. Baby animals can even imprint on people!

Why do animals use tools?

Humans are not the only creatures that use tools. Several animals use rocks and sticks to catch and eat food. To crack open a shellfish, a sea otter smashes it on a stone that it lays on its chest. Chimpanzees and finches use sticks and blades of grass to pull insects from inside trees. Elephants use sticks, but not to catch food. When held in the trunk, a stick makes a great back scratcher!

Why, oh why?

Why are some animals cannibals? An animal is a **cannibal** when it eats another of its own kind. Some animals become cannibals when food is scarce or a territory is overcrowded. Others mistake their own kind for prey.

Why do animals stick out their tongues? Snakes can sense the scent or body heat of prey with their flicking tongues. Some animals, like chameleons and frogs, stick out their tongues to catch prey. When a dog pants to cool down, it sticks out its tongue.

Why do animals shed their skin? The skin of a reptile, amphibian, spider, or insect does not grow as the animal does. When the creature grows too big for its skin, it sheds, or **molts**, the old skin to uncover a new, larger skin.

Why do some cats read? Does your cat ever lie on your homework? Usually a cat lies on your papers because it wants attention. This cat, however, works for a publishing company and is lying on a manuscript to edit mistakes.

They don't do that!

Ostriches don't stick their head in the sand to avoid danger! These birds are fierce fighters that can injure predators by kicking with their strong legs.

Bulls are **colorblind** and cannot see red. They get angry at bullfights because the crowds are very loud, and the matadors annoy them by waving a cape.

 Bats are excellent fliers that rarely crash into people's hair! They use a kind of **sonar** to guide themselves skillfully in the dark.

Words to know

animal behavior A term used to describe the actions of animals

bioluminescence A natural glow produced inside an animal's body

camouflage Patterns or colors that help an animal blend into its surroundings

cannibal An animal that eats others of its own kind

colorblind Describes an animal that cannot see a difference between colors

gland A sac inside the body that produces liquid

hibernation A winter sleep during which heart and breathing rates slow down and body temperature drops to near freezing

host An animal that is attacked by a parasite

imprint In baby animals, to fix on the appearance, scent, movements, or sound of one's parent

lantern A body organ that produces bioluminescent light

larva The wormlike baby of an insect or amphibian

migrate To move a long distance in search of food, mates, or a certain climate

mimic To act or look like an object or other animal

molt To shed skin, feathers, hair, or a shell

musk A strong-smelling liquid produced in the musk gland

parasite A creature that feeds off a living animal's blood or flesh

predator An animal that hunts and kills other animals for food

prey An animal hunted by another animal for food

scent An odor produced by an animal

sonar The use of sound waves to find the location of objects

symbiosis The helpful partnership of animals of different species

true hibernator An animal that sleeps through the winter with greatly reduced heart and breathing rates and body temperature

Index

What is in the picture?

Here is more information about the photographs in this book.

page:		page:	
front cover	Chimpanzees live in Africa.	18	The archer fish can shoot at insects from over a meter away.
title page	The Arctic ground squirrel collects grass for its winter nest.	19	Guanacos live in South America.
4-5	The tropical American basilisk escapes by running across water.	20	Click beetles are found in South America. Their lanterns look like eyes.
6	Dormice, found in Europe, are true hibernators.	21	Comb jellies inhabit all of the world's oceans and seas.
7	A North American grizzly pokes its head from its den.	22	The African elephant spends much of its time around water.
8-9	Monarch butterflies often migrate in flocks.	23	The scarab, found in Africa, is also called the dung beetle.
9	In Arctic regions, caribou migrate in search of food.	24 (top)	The rock hyrax lives in Africa and the Middle East.
10 (top)	An octopus changes color in a few seconds.	24 (bot. left)	These short-eared owlets imprint on their parents' movements.
10 (bottom)	It may take fifteen minutes for a chameleon to change color.	24 (bot. right)	This baby cuckoo has imprinted upon another species of bird.
11 (top)	The black stripes on a viceroy butterfly's wings are slightly different than on a monarch's.	26	Sea otters inhabit the coastal waters of the north Pacific.
11 (bottom)	Fireflies are actually beetles.	27	This chimpanzee uses a long blade of grass as a tool.
12-13	Opossums live in North America.	28 (left)	This bullfrog is swallowing a leopard frog.
14	Skunks live throughout Canada and the United States.	28 (right)	Rattlesnakes are native to North America.
15	The hognosed snake of North America sometimes mimics a rattlesnake.	29 (left)	This Jamaican crested anole has almost finished molting.
16	Parasites are found wherever there are hosts on which to feed.	29 (right)	Snoozer, age 8, has written many books under the pen name "Bobbie Kalman."
17 (top)	The oxpecker is often partner to the African buffalo.	30	Ostriches, found in Africa, sprint at up to 70 km/hr (45 m/hr).
17 (bottom)	An aphid excretes syrup when an ant strokes its back.		

1 2 3 4 5 6 7 8 9 0 Printed in USA 6 5 4 3 2 1 0 9 8 7